W9-BER-740

HOT AND SPICY

PHOTOGRAPHY AND DESIGN
BY KOREN TRYGG
TEXT BY LUCY POSHEK

ANTIOCH GOURMET GIFT BOOKS

Published by Antioch Publishing Company
Yellow Springs, Ohio 45387

ISBN 0-89954-825-3

HOT & SPICY

Printed and bound in the U.S.A.

Contents

INTRODUCTION

Today we use fiery foods such as chiles, garlic, onions, ginger, mustard, horseradish, and pepper to add zest and individuality to our food. They arouse our senses. They make our hearts beat faster. And, sometimes they send us an explosive jolt.

Ancient Eastern cultures were the first to use such seasonings as pepper, mustard, cloves, and cinnamon. Since most of these spices grew exclusively in the Orient, it was not until the Western world began significant exchange with the East, after the eleventh-century Crusades, that Europeans developed a voracious passion for spices.

The caravan spice-trade route from India and China through Arabia to the Mediterranean ports was a long, expensive undertaking, but by the fifteenth century, Europe was willing to pay the price. Some spices were in such high demand that they could be used in place of gold to settle debts, taxes and even ransoms.

It was the quest for more direct and economical routes to the spice-producing lands that sent Western explorers risking their lives across the Atlantic during the fifteenth and sixteenth centuries. Columbus discovered the New World while searching for spices and stumbled instead across a new kind of "pepper"—the chile—that soon put a fresh bite into cooking around the world.

Since then, from Mexico to China to India, each country has nurtured its culinary identity largely through an inventive blend of hot and spicy flavorings. And in this century, we have begun to fuse the best features of these exciting cuisines together in the search for new, ethnically mixed dishes. The results—Southwest, French-Chinese, and Cajun, to name a few—have literally become the spice of our culinary lives.

CHILE LORE

Chile peppers, or *capsicums*, belong to the same fruit family as the tomato and eggplant. The first chiles grew wild from mid-Mexico to northern Argentina. Found in ancient sites dating from 500 to 3500 B.C., chiles belong to the oldest period of domesticated agriculture in tropical America.

The early Indians used chiles in medicine, while the Aztecs discovered that chiles livened up an otherwise bland diet of squash, beans, corn and potatoes. Such dishes as tacos, tamales, guacamole, and chili powder were all originally Aztec delicacies.

When Columbus landed in the New World under the mistaken belief that he had found a direct spice route to India, he assumed the chile was black pepper because its

bite so resembled that of peppercorns. Just as the American natives were misnamed "Indians," chiles became known interchangeably as "peppers."

Chiles were introduced to Europe at a time when the poorer countries could not afford expensive Eastern spices. Here, finally, was a zesty seasoning that could be grown cheaply in the widest range of climates. Easily crossbred, hundreds of chile varieties are now cultivated throughout the world.

Chiles have traditionally been valued in hot climates as a natural thermostat. Capsaicin, the burning chemical inside chiles, encourages perspiration, resulting in a lower body temperature.

Chiles are also a high source of vitamin A and C— higher, gram for gram, than oranges, grapefruit or lemons. Many people cannot imagine consuming enough chiles to equal an orange, but in countries such as Nigeria the average adult consumes a half-pound of fresh chiles a day—just about the weight of a medium orange.

It is believed in parts of the Southern U.S. that ground-up chiles placed in the toes of one's socks will keep the feet warm.

TYPES OF CHILES

Chiles can be mild, robust, hot, or absolutely blazing, depending on the variety. Their heat is also determined by the type of soil in which they were grown, how much water they received, and whether any accidental cross-pollination occurred. These conditions all affect the burning chemicals found in chiles, the hottest of which is called *capsaicin*.

With hundreds of chile varieties now available, identifying them all is bewildering, to say the least. Since the capsaicin level in each chile can vary, many recipes simply call for red or green chiles, leaving the exact type up to the cook.

Some very general guidelines:

- The smaller and thinner the flesh of the chile, the hotter it is.
- Fresh chiles are slightly more flavorful than dried or ground ones, but canned or marinated chiles usually have the most reliably consistent potency level.
- Whether fresh, canned or dried, it is best to use chiles sparingly at first, taste often, and add more chiles or cayenne powder as needed.

The following chiles are only a sampling of some better-known varieties. In a search for bigger, milder, more flavorful chiles, new cultivars are continually appearing on the market.

Bell

Chipotle

Poblano

Habañero-dried

Ancho

Anaheim

Cascabel

Cayenne

Güero

Jalapeño

Güero

California

Serrano

Serrano—
dried

Hot to Fiery

Cayenne - Usually sold dried or powdered when red, mature, and at its hottest.

Jalapeño - Best-known chile in the United States. Canned green Jalapeños are more reliably hot than fresh ones. Also bottled *en escabeche*, or marinated.

Chipotle - Smoke-dried Jalapeño. Usually made into brown hot sauce. Favored for its hickory taste.

Pequín and Tepín - Tiny, seed-like chiles. Can be used interchangeably. Usually sold dried.

Serrano - A bit hotter than the Jalapeño. Usually used fresh.

Thai - Widely found in Oriental markets in all forms. Used for any dish where intense but not lingering heat is desired.

Habañero - Grown in Mexico, this is the hottest pepper in the world.

Fairly Hot

Pasilla - Earthy-tasting. Known as Chilaca when fresh, Negro when dried.

Cascabel - Its name means jingle bell, as its seeds rattle when dry. Nutty flavor.

Hungarian Yellow Wax - Sweet variety is sold as the Banana Pepper and the hot variety as the Yellow Wax Pepper.

Sandia - Good *relleno* chile, especially for those who like more heat than the mild varieties provide. Can be roasted and peeled when green, or ripened and hung in

ristras, or dried and ground for hot red chile powder.

Güero - Used fresh or pickled. Similar to Hungarian Yellow Wax.

Mild

Anaheim - One of the best stuffing chiles. Must be roasted and peeled if used fresh and green. Sold in canned, dried or powder form. Also known as New Mexico.

Mulato - Favorite *mole* chile in Mexico. Toasty chocolate flavor, similar to Ancho and Poblano. Usually sold dried.

California - Dried cultivar of the Anaheim. Good all-purpose chile. Also sold powdered. Often used for stringing in *ristras* since the skin is smoother than most dried red chiles.

Poblano - Another good *relleno* chile. Shaped almost like a valentine.

Ancho - Dried Poblano. Spicy, with slight apple flavor.

Bell Peppers - Sweet members of the *capsicum* family but without the capsaicin. Available in red, yellow, green and purple-black colors, the latter two tasting slightly less sweet. Roasted, stored and peeled like chile peppers. Used often for stuffing.

Paprika - Variety of sweet red pepper, but smaller and more piquant. Cultivated in Hungary, the well-known powder seasoning is a distinctive feature of Hungarian cooking. The "hot" Hungarian paprika has only about one-tenth the power of cayenne.

PREPARING CHILES

Acommon fallacy is that the seeds are the hottest part of a chile. The heat is actually in the membrane and veins to which the seeds are attached. For a milder flavor, remove the membrane and seeds.

It is best to wear plastic gloves when handling hot chiles. Capsaicin is hard to wash off your hands and can be very painful if it comes in contact with the eyes, nose or mouth.

Fresh, canned and dried chiles should all be rinsed in cold water before preparing.

Preparing fresh or canned chiles: Unless making *chiles rellenos* (in which case the seeds and veins should be removed but the stem left intact), cut away the stem, split the chile open, and scrape away the veins and seeds with a knife on a flat surface. To make them less hot, soak prepared chiles in cold water for one hour.

Preparing dried chiles: Cut chiles into small pieces with a knife or scissors. To soften the chiles for use in a sauce, soak them in hot water for an hour or until pliable.

Roasting: The skins of some fresh chiles and sweet peppers can be removed with a vegetable peeler—especially if their skins are thick—but roasting is the preferred method. This can be done in a broiler, on an outdoor

grill, or speared on a fork over a gas burner. (Some cooks even recommend a blowtorch!) The key is to turn the chiles often, blistering all sides of the pepper evenly until the skin is well charred, but the flesh underneath is still firm. Steam the roasted peppers in a paper bag or cloth towel for ten minutes so the skins peel away more easily.

"The man that eats no pepper is weak.
Pepper is the staff of life."

WEST AFRICAN PROVERB

17

DRYING CHILES

Drying chiles is most easily done in arid climates. Fully mature long red or yellow chiles are strung into clusters called *ristras* and hung in the sun to dry. *Ristras* are a colorful sign of welcome in the American Southwest.

To make a *ristra*, tie a knot in the end of a strong length of string. Using a carpet needle, puncture each chile just below the stem and thread the chiles together, leaving no gaps between the stems. Hang them wherever warm air circulates. Once dry, store the chiles in sealed containers or hang in the kitchen. If you leave them hanging outside, they should be kept away from the direct sun. In dry climates, they can last a year or two.

You can also dry chiles by spreading them in the sun on well-ventilated screens or baskets. Drying takes three or four days of bright even sun. If the humidity is over thirty percent, the chiles must be brought in at night.

If living in an area with uneven sunshine, low temperatures or high humidity, try hanging *ristras* inside, with several hours of sunlight per day. After a week, finish drying them in a very low oven until leathery but not brittle.

Hot & Spicy Potpourri

2 cups (16 fl. oz.) dried red chiles
1 cup (8 fl. oz.) dried Jamaica Roja chiles (optional)
¼ cup (2 fl. oz.) each bay and sage leaves
¼ cup (2 fl. oz.) dried lemon peel
1¼ cup (10 fl. oz.) wood shavings, pods and dried leaves
2 tbsp. (1½ Br. tbsp.) whole cloves, crushed slightly
1 tbsp. (¾ Br. tbsp.) whole allspice, crushed slightly
2 tbsp. (1½ Br. tbsp.) dried crushed chile flakes
5 whole cinnamon sticks, crushed slightly
2 tbsp. (1½ Br. tbsp.) gum benzoin   8 drops chile oil

Combine all ingredients. Store in a covered container in a cool place for 6 to 8 weeks, stirring or shaking every other day.

19

PEPPERCORNS

The *piper nigrum* was once a rare, expensive condiment valued as a remarkable preservative and flavoring. In medieval society a pound of pepper was worth a pound of gold.

The most common types of pepper are all from the same climbing vine, with berries that ripen from green to red to brown. **Black pepper** is obtained from unripened, sun-dried berries; **white pepper** is from fully ripe berries with their outer husks removed; **green peppers**, popular in *nouvelle cuisine*, are unripe berries that are dried, pickled, or canned; **grey pepper** is a mixture of white and black pepper.

White peppercorns have only a slightly milder flavor than black and are often favored in white sauces. Mashed, pickled green peppercorns are handy when a softer texture is desired.

Whole peppercorns keep their flavor longer than ground pepper in storage, but they must be crushed to release their essence in cooking.

"Pepper is small in quantity and great in virtue."
PLATO

SPICY SPICES

Allspice, also known as Jamaican pepper, is grown mostly in Jamaica. The berries have an exotic taste of cinnamon, cloves and nutmeg combined. Used whole for marinades and pickling; ground in meatballs, cakes and breads. Best bought whole and ground fresh.

Cardamom, of the ginger family, grows green husks whose seeds are dried and sold whole or ground. Much used in its native India for flavoring rice, sweets, omelettes, meats and noodles. In Arabia, whole cardamom seeds are a delicious addition to Turkish coffee.

Cloves are the dried, unopened, reddish-brown flower buds of a tropical East Indian evergreen tree. They keep exceptionally well whether ground or whole. Their strong fragrance adds a pungent taste to hams, meats, stews, soups, curries, and cakes.

Coriander is the seed of a plant whose leaves are used as an herb, but the flavor of the seed—sweetly cumin-like—is quite different. A principal ingredient in curry and *garam masala*. Also used in sausages and other meats.

Cumin has a pungent, nutty flavor often found in the cuisines of India, Mexico, and the American Southwest. Black cumin is a darker, more delicately-flavored variety found mostly in Indian stores. Best bought in seed form, then ground up fresh.

Turmeric, a root of the ginger family, is grown in the tropics. Available only in ground form, turmeric adds a rich, saffron-like golden color and rather biting taste to foods. A main ingredient in mustards, curries, sauces, and pickles. Should be used sparingly.

MUSTARD

Native to the Mediterranean, mustard has been used in foods and medicines since ancient times. It is most commonly grown in wine-producing regions where it serves as a regenerative crop between the rows of vines.

There are several mustard seed varieties: white or yellow, brown, and black. The darker their color, the hotter they are. The seeds are sold whole, powdered, and as a prepared sauce. Since mustard blends so well with other condiments and flavorings, endless variations— honey, champagne, ale, red wine, and even raspberry mustards—have been created.

The flavor of mustard fades rapidly once moisture is added or a bottle is opened. A slice of lime added to the bottle helps preserve mustard.

An easy fresh mustard sauce can be made by mixing 2 or 3 tbsp. (1½-2¼ Br. tbsp.) water or vinegar with ¼ cup (2 fl. oz.) dry mustard. In French kitchens, a traditional sauce is made with crushed mustard seeds, a little white wine and oil.

Flavored Mustards

Per cup (8 fl. oz.) of prepared mustard add:
Raspberry Mustard—*Gently fold in ¹/₂ cup (4 fl. oz.) fresh raspberries. Sweeten to taste with honey.*
Peppercorn Mustard—*Add 2 tbsp. (1¹/₂ Br. tbsp.) partially crushed mixed peppercorns.*
Garlic Mustard—*Add ¹/₄ cup (2 fl. oz.) coarse ground mustard seed and 2 cloves fresh garlic, minced.*
Herb Mustard—*Mix any combination of basil, dill, tarragon and thyme together, equalling 6 tsp. (4¹/₂ Br. tsp.) fresh herbs, or 3 tsp. (2¹/₄ Br. tsp.) dried herbs.*

GINGER

The fibrous, spicy root of the ginger plant is the only hot flavoring that can complement both sweet and savory dishes. Traditionally known as the seasoning in gingerbread, its refreshing taste brings out the best in meat and poultry and also diminishes fishy odors. The herb is sold in a great variety of forms—fresh, powdered, candied, and pickled, to name a few.

Considered essential in cleansing the body and soul, gingerroot is widely used in Eastern herbal remedies and cooking. It prevents motion sickness, acts as an analgesic and antioxidant, stimulates the immune system, and helps lower cholesterol. Ginger tea has a warm, soothing effect on coughs and colds. Throughout Asia, pickled ginger is often eaten between each course.

Fresh ginger keeps well in a dry place or in the freezer. But the best method of preservation is to peel the root and refrigerate it in a jar of sherry. It will not only keep indefinitely this way without soaking up the flavor or alcohol of the sherry, but the flavored sherry can later be used in cooking.

The root is usually peeled, then sliced or grated. A one-inch piece yields about two teaspoons (1½ Br. tsp.) of grated ginger.

HORSERADISH

Horseradish is not a radish at all, but rather more closely related to mustard. Like mustard, it has a sharp, pungent taste that assails the sinuses and should be used sparingly.

Applied externally or inhaled, grated horseradish is said to stimulate circulation and relieve congestion. The herb also aids the digestion of fatty foods and serves well as a marinade and tenderizing agent.

Bottled and powdered horseradishes are widely avail-

able, but the fresh root, peeled and grated, is most potent. Adding a bit of fresh horseradish to whipped or sour cream creates a classic sauce for canapés and cold meats.

Japanese *wasabi*, a green root that is most often seen in paste form accompanying *sushi* and *sashimi*, is a close relative of common horseradish.

GARLIC AND ONIONS

Of all the *Allium* herbs and members of the lily family—garlic, onions, shallots, leeks, and chives—probably no other food has been revered more than **garlic.** Referred to throughout history as "nature's miracle medicine chest," the virtues of garlic are many: Recent studies suggest that it may help lower blood pressure and cholesterol levels, strengthen the immune system, and protect against carcinogens.

A garlic bulb consists of 12-16 cloves, each protected by a parchment-like skin. To loosen the skins, blanch the cloves briefly, or crush them with the bottom of a jar or the flat side of a cutting knife.

To tone down the taste of garlic, sauté the cloves or simmer them in water before cooking, or remove the harsh-tasting inner green part of the cloves. Using whole cloves yields the mildest flavor whereas pressed garlic is the strongest.

Onions, rich in sulphur and vitamin C, have been a mainstay of cooking for more than five thousand years. Among the **yellow** onions are the sweet Spanish, Egyptian, Polish, and French varieties. **Pickling** or **button** onions can be added whole to dishes. **White** onions are classic cooking onions, whereas **pink** and **red** onions are best raw.

While the **leek** is a favorite soup onion, **shallots** are preferred for delicate sauces. Only the leaves of **chives** are usually used to flavor food.

Scallions, or green onions, are very versatile in the kitchen: they add a mild flavor to long-cooking dishes (tied into a knot for easy removal), make a wonderful garnish for soups and salads, and can be eaten raw.

To peel onions without tears, peel them under running water or pre-refrigerate them for an hour. Onion odor on the hands can be removed with salt, vinegar, lemon juice, or powdered mustard.

The best antidotes to garlic and onion breath are raw parsley, fennel seeds, or other greens, brushing your teeth with salt, or sucking on a lemon.

"Life itself is like an onion: it has a bewildering number of layers; you peel them off, one by one, and sometimes you cry."

CARL SANDBURG

Oyster Shooters

8 shucked oysters
seafood cocktail sauce

grated horseradish
lemon wedges

Drop each oyster into a separate shot glass and spoon a layer of cocktail sauce on top. Sprinkle with grated horseradish and serve with a lemon wedge. Can be eaten with a crab fork or downed straight from the glass like a shot. Serves 4-8 as an appetizer.

Garlic Mashed Potatoes

4 medium russet potatoes, peeled
4 tbsp. (3 Br. tbsp.) butter
1 whole head of garlic, roasted
½ cup (4 fl. oz.) half and half (half cream, half whole
    milk), warmed
½ cup (4 fl. oz.) sour cream
salt and pepper to taste

Wrap unpeeled head of garlic in foil and cook in 400°F oven for 25-30 minutes. Then peel. Meanwhile, boil potatoes until tender. Drain well. Over low heat, mash potatoes. Add butter and garlic and mix well. Add half and half and sour cream. Season to taste with salt and pepper. Serve immediately. Serves 4.

Salsa

1 pound ripe red tomatoes
2 tbsp. (1½ Br. tbsp.)
  chopped onions, optional
3 cloves garlic,
  peeled and minced

¼ cup (2 fl. oz.) fresh
  cilantro, chopped
1 small whole fresh jalapeño
  or serrano pepper, sliced
2 tsp. (1½ Br. tsp.) lime juice
¼ tsp. salt

Remove seeds from tomatoes and cut into small pieces. Set aside onions and half the tomatoes. Place other half of tomatoes and remaining ingredients into a food processor and mix 3-5 seconds. Strain excess liquid. Stir in onions and remaining tomatoes.

Chile Corn Bread Muffins

2 tbsp. (1½ Br. tbsp.) butter
1⅓ cups (10⅔ fl. oz.)
  cornmeal
⅓ cup (2⅔ fl. oz.) flour
3 tbsp. (2¼ Br. tbsp.) sugar
1 tsp. (¾ Br. tsp.) salt

1 tsp. (¾ Br. tsp.) baking soda
2 cups (16 fl. oz.) milk
1 cup (8 fl. oz.) buttermilk
2 eggs
2 oz. diced jalapeño chiles
2 oz. diced Ortega chiles

Place butter in a square baking pan and melt in preheating oven for a few minutes. In large bowl, sift the dry ingredients together. Stir in 1 cup of milk and buttermilk, then the eggs and chiles. Pour batter into hot muffin pan and carefully top it with remaining 1 cup milk. Do not stir. Bake at 400°F for 35 minutes. Serves 6 to 8.

Shown clockwise from the top:
Vegetarian Chili, Salsa,
Chile Corn Bread Muffins and Chiles Rellenos

Chiles Rellenos

8 whole green roasted chiles, fresh or canned
  (fresh chiles tend to be hotter)
Monterey Jack or mozzarella cheese, cut into sticks
4 eggs, separated
4 tbsp. (3 Br. tbsp.) flour, plus flour for dredging
1 tsp. (¾ Br. tsp.) baking powder
1 tbsp. (¾ Br. tbsp.) water
¼ tsp. salt
lots of paper towels
frying oil

Wash chiles, removing their seeds and veins. Pat fairly dry, then dredge them in flour until completely dusted. Stuff cheese sticks carefully inside chiles. (Try to avoid tearing the skins.) Set aside.

Beat egg whites until stiff. In separate bowl, combine egg yolks (slightly beaten with a fork), baking powder, water, flour and salt. Fold egg yolk mixture into egg whites.

Dip chiles into batter until well-coated and fry them in a half-inch of oil, one or two at a time, turning until lightly browned. Remove and drain chiles on paper towels. Serve immediately. Can top with red salsa, if desired, and accompany with rice and beans. Serves 4.

Counteracting Fiery Chiles

Starchy foods and dairy products, such as milk, yogurt, sour cream, bread, rice, and tortillas can help put out the fire from hot chiles. Capsaicin is most soluble in alcohol, so beer or tequila may cool your mouth better than water.

Vegetarian Chili

1 cup (8 fl. oz.) each small dried red beans and black beans
2 large cans Italian plum tomatoes, cut up
3 cloves garlic, chopped
1 large dried California or pasilla chile, washed and seeded
1 chopped onion
1 chopped green bell pepper
1 cup (8 fl. oz.) each sliced carrots and celery
1 tsp. (¾ Br. tsp.) cumin
chili powder and crushed red peppers to taste
1 bay leaf

*Presoak beans, if desired, or simply wash them.
Add all ingredients to pot and cover well with water.
Simmer 2-4 hours (or more) until beans are tender.
Remove chile skin before serving.*

*"Chili is much improved by having had a
day to contemplate its fate."*

JOHN STEELE GORDON

Angry Pasta

3 tbsp. (2¼ Br. tbsp.) olive oil
4-6 oz. prosciutto
4 cloves garlic, minced
1 medium white onion, chopped
4 red chile peppers, chopped (seeds removed)
¼ cup (2 fl. oz.) fresh oregano, minced
⅓ cup (2⅔ fl. oz.) fresh basil, minced
1 6-ounce can tomato paste
¾ cup (6 fl. oz.) red wine
3-4 whole tomatoes, chopped
1 12-ounce package penne pasta, cooked
⅓ cup (2⅔ fl. oz.) grated Parmesan cheese
⅓ cup (2⅔ fl. oz.) grated Romano cheese

Sauté prosciutto in oil until crisp and remove. Use renderings to sauté onion, garlic, red pepper, oregano and basil. Add tomato paste and wine and cook on medium heat for 10 minutes. Add tomatoes and cook until tender. Season to taste. In large bowl, toss cooked penne with sauce. Add Romano cheese and half of the Parmesan cheese. Toss well. Sprinkle crumbled prosciutto and remaining Parmesan cheese on top. Serves 4.

Pictured on the previous page: Creole Scampi and Angry Pasta

Creole Scampi

1 pound large fresh shrimp (prawns), peeled
3 tbsp. (2¼ Br. tbsp.) olive oil
3 tbsp. (2¼ Br. tbsp.) butter
1½ cups (12 fl. oz.) white wine
½ cup (4 fl. oz.) lemon juice
4 tsp. (3 Br. tsp.) garlic, crushed
3 tsp. (2¼ Br. tsp.) crushed red pepper
1 tsp. (¾ Br. tsp.) cayenne pepper
2 tsp. (1½ Br. tsp.) black pepper
¼ cup (2 fl. oz.) chopped parsley

In a skillet melt butter in olive oil. Add wine, lemon juice, garlic, and red, cayenne and black pepper. Cook over medium heat until bubbles appear. Add shrimp and cook over high heat, turning frequently. Deglaze the pan, reducing remaining liquid to a sauce. Serve over rice with French bread for dipping. Garnish with fresh chopped parsley. Serves 4.

"A nickel will get you on the subway, but garlic will get you a seat."

OLD YIDDISH PROVERB

Curry

¾ cup (6 fl. oz.) chopped onions
3 cloves minced garlic
2 tbsp. (1½ Br. tbsp.) butter
¼ tsp. minced fresh ginger
3 tbsp. (2¼ Br. tbsp.) tomato paste
½ tsp. salt
2 tbsp. (1½ Br. tbsp.) lemon juice
2 tbsp. (1½ Br. tbsp.) flour
4 cups (32 fl. oz.) water
curry powder (next page)

Sauté onions and garlic in butter until soft, about 5 minutes. Add ginger, tomato paste, salt, lemon juice, flour, curry powder and water. Stir well over low flame. Add vegetables and/or meat.
Beef*—tri-tip roast cut into 2-inch cubes*
Chicken*—boneless and skinless is best*
Vegetables*—mushrooms, potatoes, cauliflower, carrots, peas, etc.*
When done, serve with rice. Best second day.

"Too hot...my teeth are melting."

WOODY ALLEN
(upon tasting a hot curry)

Curry Powder

3 tbsp. (2¼ Br. tbsp.) coriander powder
2 tbsp. (1½ Br. tbsp.) ground cumin
2 tbsp. (1½ Br. tbsp.) turmeric powder
1 tbsp. (¾ Br. tbsp.) chile powder
1 tsp. (¾ Br. tsp.) celery seed
1 tsp. (¾ Br. tsp.) ground red pepper or to taste
1 tsp. (¾ Br. tsp.) dry mustard
½ tsp. ground mace
½ tsp. ground cinnamon
¼ tsp. white pepper
fresh ground pepper to taste
⅛ tsp. cardamom seeds

Ginger Chicken Stir-Fry

1 pound boneless, skinless chicken, cut into cubes
2 tsp. (1½ Br. tsp.) fresh ginger, peeled and grated
2 cups (16 fl. oz.) shredded cabbage
1 cup (8 fl. oz.) sliced celery
2 tsp. (1½ Br. tsp.) crushed red pepper, or as desired
2 tbsp. (1½ Br. tbsp.) soy sauce
2 tsp. (1½ Br. tsp.) sugar or honey
2 tbsp. (1½ Br. tbsp.) sherry
2 tbsp. (1½ Br. tbsp.) oil
¼ cup (2 fl. oz.) chicken broth
2 tbsp. (1½ Br. tbsp.) cornstarch mixed with
    ¼ cup (2 fl. oz.) water
½ cup (4 fl. oz.) green onions, chopped

Mix together soy sauce, sugar and sherry. Marinate cubed chicken in mixture while preparing other ingredients.

Stir-fry chicken in oil until browned, then remove with slotted spoon. Add crushed red peppers (if you want it fiery), ginger, cabbage and celery to pan, and stir-fry for 2 minutes. Return chicken to pan, add broth, and slowly stir in cornstarch mixture until sauce thickens. Add green onions last. Serve with rice. Serves 4.

Spicy Prawn & Noodle Soup

12-15 large prawns (shrimp)
4 cups (32 fl. oz.) chicken stock
½ cup (4 fl. oz.) water
2 tsp. (1½ Br. tsp.) coriander seeds
1 tsp. (¾ Br. tsp.) peppercorns
1-2 jalapeño chiles, sliced
2 tsp. (1½ Br. tsp.) chopped garlic
½ cup (4 fl. oz.) sliced green onions
4-8 dried or fresh mushrooms; shiitaki, straw or oyster
2 ounces bean starch noodles
fresh cilantro for garnishing

In a large saucepan heat chicken stock to a medium boil. Add prawns and simmer for 2 minutes. Turn off heat and allow to cool for 4 minutes. Remove prawns. Reheat stock and stir in water, chiles, garlic and green onions. Tie peppercorns and coriander seeds into a cheesecloth packet and add to water. Add mushrooms and noodles and simmer until noodles are done. Remove cheesecloth packet. Add prawns and serve garnished with cilantro if desired. Serves 4.

Shown in center:
Ginger Chicken Stir-Fry
On the left: Spicy Prawn & Noodle Soup